Before The Mirror
A collection of thought-provoking poems

MIKE O NWANGWA

authorHOUSE®

AuthorHouse™ UK
1663 Liberty Drive
Bloomington, IN 47403 USA
www.authorhouse.co.uk
Phone: 0800 047 8203 (Domestic TFN)
   +44 1908 723714 (International)

© 2019 Mike O Nwangwa. All rights reserved.

No part of this book may be reproduced, stored in a retrieval system, or transmitted by any means without the written permission of the author.

Published by AuthorHouse 09/20/2019

ISBN: 978-1-7283-9364-3 (sc)
ISBN: 978-1-7283-9365-0 (e)

Print information available on the last page.

Any people depicted in stock imagery provided by Getty Images are models, and such images are being used for illustrative purposes only.
Certain stock imagery © Getty Images.

This book is printed on acid-free paper.

Because of the dynamic nature of the Internet, any web addresses or links contained in this book may have changed since publication and may no longer be valid. The views expressed in this work are solely those of the author and do not necessarily reflect the views of the publisher, and the publisher hereby disclaims any responsibility for them.

Dedication

To the love of my life, Crystal

Introduction

Mirrors are very beneficial. Standing before a mirror is not new to you, I believe. We use the mirror because we want change. We want the mirror to show us our flaws: the part of our dressing that needs to be corrected, that unbuttoned shirt, uncombed hair, not-too-bright eyes etc.

The mirror points to our flaws in order for us to take care of them. Afterwards, we emerge to the public as confident, happy people.

This book is intended to work like a mirror. Infact it is one! What you are about to explore is a compendium of some of my favorite poems, written over time. They are an expression of my heart, covering different issues of life. You will come across serious truths presented with a blend of humor, sarcasm, inspiration and wittiness. They are written in modern day language so many of us can follow. Besides, as you read, you'll find yourself identifying with several characters in the poems. I hope this book blesses you.

Reading this book will be fun I promise you. Just remember, it works like a mirror. It can only show you your flaws, but won't do anything to correct them. You are responsible for the necessary change in your life. I challenge you to do something about the imperfections you will notice as you stand…*before the mirror.*

Mike o Nwangwa

Suffering and Smiling

They pinch me today. I wince, and then I smile
They slap me today. I stagger, then I smile
I am pushed to the wall. My back hits the wall with a thud. Then I smile
Though the smile be painful, still I smile.

They conspire against me, I am awe-struck, but I smile
My one true love jilted me. I am heart-broken, yet I smile
The man in the Peugeot just bashed my Matrix. I am angry, still I smile
Though the smile be forced. I still smile.

My wallet is missing with my valuables. With a deep sense of loss, I smile
The creditor is at my door. I am under the bed and I smile
My fortunes are dwindling. I am depressed, yet I smile
Though the smile is not external, deep within, I smile.

I won't let my circumstances influence my mien
Instead my attitude will influence my situation
No matter what happens, I'll smile
For what happens to me is not as important as what happens in me
So with an air of finality, I smile.

Ignorance

Behold a queen
Sitting on a throne
Yet she knows it not
With land so rich
And culture so deep
Yet she knows it not

All hail the heir
With all claim to the estate
Yet he knows it not
He strolls by hungrily
When he's not slaving
Yet his wealth wastes away
And he languishes in penury

Deprivation, hunger and impoverishment
Await the queen, the heir, royalty
Who though are blessed with riches
And have the keys to wealth
Know it not, for ignorance.

No Hurry in Life

I was travelling the other day
The vehicle was slow, I was turning grey
It was quite irksome, or so I thought
To be faced with such a lot.
Soon a vehicle pulled in ahead of me.
"No hurry in life" on it I could see
That was the last thing I needed to hear
For I felt I was so close to the rear

Several times we feel that way
We really would fly if we had a say
But God has a plan for everyman
And such plans differ from John to Dan
What if we went faster
And ended up in the hall of disaster?
God sees ahead of you
And He'll surely see you through

I suggest you discover your purpose
And resist all that oppose
Stop comparing yourself with another
Or else you might become a goner

We all have different lives to live
And friend, you have the best to give
Some get there quite early and others later
But then the former will bow to the latter.

Stop complaining that you're too slow
Rather purpose in your heart to row
Until you get to the top, the very peak
Even though many thought you were too weak
You'll get there, I know you will
And thereafter, your wounds will heal

Take A Step

Sometimes you may wonder why
In spite of all your plans
Things don't work out your way.
I'll tell you what—take a step.

You may have prayed about something
Or thought about it for so long
If the problem seems to linger
Then you need to take a step

If an athlete covets the world record
Or a student aims for excellence
It's not enough to think, wish and pray.
It's expedient they take a step.

You may enjoy wallowing in the pleasure
Of your plans for the future
You won't go far at all
Except you take a step

Your goals may seem so hard to reach
The road to success may seem so long
But doubtless, you can shorten it
If you start by taking a step

Many great men started small
Don't sit and wait, do something now
Gradually, but steadily you'll get there
Just ensure you take a step.

Sandra Sally Stalwart

One sunny Sunday, at sunrise on the seventh of September, Sixteen sixty six, Sandra Sally Stalwart sang songs specifically for southern sailors setting sail southwards. Sandy Sammy Stalwart, Sandra's spouse smiled seemingly satisfied at Sandra's songs of salutation sung for southern sailors. Sadly, Stephanie, Sandra's step sister shouted "stop! I submit Sandra's songs are somewhat soporific, stirring me to sleep."

Sandra stopped singing songs. She was saddened at Stephanie's sadistic sarcasm. Stephanie succeeded in smashing Sandra's spirit that Sunday. Sandra was so saddened that at sunset of Sunday Seventeenth September, Sixteen sixty six, Sandra sang her swansong. Spear-mouthed Stephanie had stifled her to senselessness. Shalom Sandra. Surely your sweet soul shall sleep in soundness.

The Log and the Speck

I saw a speck in my neighbor's eye
An ugly, irritating, tiny-yet-deadly speck
So I screamed at him
"Get rid of that speck!"
"You wretched sinner," I continued, "that speck is evil"
But he just smiled, pointed towards my eye and
Mumbled something I didn't hear.

I was a total adherent to the law
I never committed adultery, though I had immoral thoughts.
I never cheated, though I benefitted
From those who did.
I never killed, though I refused to help the dying.
I never stole, yet I was stingy—both to God and man.
I thought I must be almost perfect.

But one day, I looked in the mirror
And lodged in both my eyes were well
Fashioned logs. They seemed to be custom made.
For they fitted my eyes perfectly
Poor me! I had always seen specks in people's eyes
While I carried logs in mine

Logs of hypocrisy, ignorance, self righteousness
And pride they were.
My logs made me critical and overbearing on people
I only saw their weaknesses and not their strengths.

The good news is that when I called out to God
In humility and repentance
Those logs were taken out and I clearly saw
I am now a brand new man
I have been reborn
My neighbor's speck is still there
But I see it differently now
Rather than yell, "You are a sinner!"
I simply help him take the speck out.

Saving the Best for Tomorrow.

He was saving his best for tomorrow
So he didn't do his best today.
He thought to himself:
'I could always do a casual job
Today and put in my last ounce of
Strength tomorrow.'
So he kept at his work
Doing the job of an average man
All because he was saving his best for tomorrow.

But tomorrow for him never came because he
Died today.
And he died a mediocrity
The world never got to know of his best
Because he didn't do it today.
He was saving it for tomorrow
So he died unsung, unmourned, unmissed
Because nobody knew him
Nobody knows mediocrities
They only know the best.

Are you saving your best for tomorrow
And not doing your best today?
Learn to give your best today
Or else you never will.
For when tomorrow comes
There'll be another tomorrow
For which you'll want to save your best again.
And this could go on for a whole lifetime.

Worse, tomorrow for you may never come
If you die today
Then the world will never get to know of your best
Because you didn't do it today.
You were saving it for tomorrow.
Do not die unsung, unmourned, Unmissed and unknown.
Nobody knows the best of tomorrow,
They only know the best of today.

The Valley of Decision

I was sleeping in that valley
That dark, damp, demoralizing vale
Everywhere, people around me seemed to
Be climbing higher…out of the valley
Making headway in life
But there was poor little me
In the valley of decision.

I was sitting in that valley
That dangerous, debilitating, distracting vale
Every other person seemed to know where they
Were going
On my part, I was waiting for the right time
To make up my mind
To make my move
But I had started waiting for that opportunity
Twelve years earlier
Alas! There was miserable little me
Still in the valley of decision.

I was standing in the valley
That dirty, dreary, demonized vale
I had begun to see what a fool I was
One bold decision, one bold move
Could have taken me higher than I was
My friends had soared on to the mountains
Though we all were once in the valley.
So it was, at last, hopeful, little me
Wanting out of the valley of decision.

So I climbed out of that valley
That desolate, deserted, deleterious vale
Higher and higher I climbed
As I boldly made a decision here
And took a bold step there
It wasn't as hard as I thought
I had made mountains out of my valleys
So I thought I could never climb out.
But not only did I climb out of that valley,
I climbed to the peak of a mountain.
That's where I still am today.

As long as you don't decide
You'll always be beside
And when others would have reached the peak
There'll still be poor little you
Crouching in the valley of decision.

Great Faith

I'll tell you the story of 'Faith-full' Felix
Who had great faith but lacked the works
He'd sit down all day and boast to us:
One day I will go to Sydney, Rome, and Venice
None dared challenge him
Lest we be said to have no faith
But while we worked hard with zest and vim
Felix did no work but wait on faith.

How would one eat if he does not work?
How would one be rich without working for it?
But Felix, 'Mr. Faith-full' would not hear of it
He'd rather let his faith do the work.
He'd fast and pray and groan and wail
Felix was getting it all wrong
For faith without works is sure to fail
Such faith isn't much better than cow dung

Today, I make this known to you
I've been to Sydney, Rome, and Venice
But my dear 'Faith-full' Felix
Has had to start life anew

After years of faith without works
He's just now learning to do it right
Life has given him a few knocks
All because of his folly. Sorry plight.

Felix never got to cross
The nearest river to our village
But now he knows faith is just a visual image
Of your desires, goals and course
Faith will help you focus on your desires
But without works, faith is sterile and dead
Works are all your faith requires
to make it from point A to Z.

Popular But Not Great.

We often mistake popular for great
Just like we mistake an empty boast
For faith.
But just as night is different from day
So popularity and greatness differ in every way

To be popular is just to be known
Whether for good or evil by everyone
But the great are those who have shown
Others the path to greatness, one by one.

The popular may soon be forgotten after
They're gone
For the thrill they once produced often dies
With them
But the great are never forgotten even
When they're worn
For they have lived to make out of every
Being, a rare gem.

Greatness is measured by your impact on lives
And not by what men think of you
But you could be popular and end up in the archives
What I tell you now is really true.

Journey Back Home

I've strayed so far from home
Like a fugitive, now I roam
My family I left to be on my own
But away like a bird, the riches have flown.

I left daddy because I'm grown.
I need no counsel, this is my zone
I spent my money, just to be known
But now, with money gone, I stand alone.

I hunger, I thirst, I'm totally broke.
I'm dying, I'm crying, please break the yoke
I'll go back to daddy. This is no joke.
I'm covered in shame, as if it were smoke.

I started for home, to plead with dad
I saw him from afar. His visage was sad
He waited every day for me, in sack cloth clad.
Now I was back. He was so glad

Blown Away

Blown away
By the wind of mercy
My sins, my faults
Into the sea of forgetfulness
No condemnation
No accusations
Just grace, mercy, forgiveness
No more haunting shadows
From the ugly past.
No more painful regrets
From my straying of yesterday
All I feel now is peace
Uncontested, inexplicable peace.

No condemnation
No accusations
Case dismissed.
Discharged and acquitted.
My sins have been blown away.

Mr Right

Two men went to work on the farm.
"This soil is sandy", said one of them
"No it is loamy", said the other
"You are wrong, I am right", said the first
"I am right, you are wrong", retorted the other
They argued all day and didn't get the work done.

Two students were preparing for a test
"Twelve times twelve is one hundred", said one of them
"No, I think it is twenty four", said the other
"You are wrong, I am right", said the first.
"I am right, you are wrong", screamed the other.
Well, they were both wrong.
But neither of them thought he could be wrong.
So they didn't bother to seek another opinion.
They were both convinced of their infallibility, their impeccability.
Oh! The test? Well, they both failed.

Two doctors were discussing a case
"He has a benign growth on his lower lip"
"No, I think it's a malignant one", said the other

"You are wrong, I am right", said the first.
"I am right, you are wrong", bellowed the other.
On and on they argued. They were both sure of themselves and none would step down for the other.
Did you ask about investigations?
Who remembers that during an argument?
Each was bent on proving his mettle.
The patient died shortly afterwards while they were still yelling
At each other
If only one of them had accepted he could be wrong…

Two children were on their way to school
"Look at that long rope", said Obi
"No it is a snake", Audu replied.
"I said it's a rope, can't you see?" yelled Obi
"You must be blind. It's a snake", responded Audu.
They argued to the point of fighting
For pugnacious boys they were.
Both were convinced they were right and didn't
mind fighting to prove it.
Audu pushed Obi and slam!!!
He fell on a sharp stone that cut him badly.

What a sight! Blood gushed out uncontrollably
It might interest you to know that it was a rope they saw.
But what did it matter at that point? Someone had been injured badly.
What a silly thing to fight over.

But aren't we often like that?
We argue just to show we are right.
But leave the work to suffer.
If we must succeed as a team
Then it doesn't matter who is right or who is wrong.
Who is smarter or who is duller.
All that matters is that we put our heads together, brood over our
Ideas together and fabricate new things.
If we work together, we'll all be called winners.

Never seek to always be right.
If you do, you will lose many friends.
If you do, the work will suffer.
How would you like to be declared?
Mr. Right
Yet be an utter failure in all your labors.

Forgot to Remember

I usually forget to remember important things
But somehow I remember to forget them
I need to remember motivational things
And forget bad things
Forget the pains, regrets, hurts of the past

As long as I do not forget the negative
Then I'll always forget to remember things that matter.
For my head and mind would have been clogged already
With the junk I forgot to forget

Work Now!

They hated work. They loved to swim
All of them except for Jim
They swam, they screamed, they laughed, they ducked
But Jim, my friend, stayed home and worked

Today, my friend Jim is very rich
He has carved out for himself a niche
The other folks are not like him
For while he worked, they chose to swim

Jim can now afford a pool at home
His house looks like a mighty dome
Now his lazy friends will tell you better
"Work now and swim later"

Father Frederick Ford

One Friday, in Finland, Fifty five followers of Frederick Ford found four foreigners freezing. Five fanatical followers frantically frowned at the fifty for freeing the four fortunate foreigners from "frosty", the freezer's firm fist.

Frederick Ford, Father of fathers, fed the four fortunate foreigners for forty four Fridays with fried fish and fresh fruits. The four famished foreigners found favor with Father Frederick Ford.

From fourth of February fourteen forty four, the four foreigners fed and freed by Father Frederick Ford and his fifty followers flooded frosty Finland with fleshy fowls for fatherly father Frederick. Four friendly favors surely facilitate another.

Be Patient

Sometimes I feel like jumping out of my skin….
Like slowing down time so I could be faster than it
But deep within, I hear that voice: "Be Patient."

I get agitated when others get ahead of me
Almost feel like overtaking them
Just to show them that I'm no pushover
But deep within, I hear that voice: "Be Patient."

That boy was in Secondary School when I finished University
But now he's driving an SUV….
Cruising round town as though he owned all the roads
But here I am cruising on my feet
And with each revolution of his tyres, my heart pounds with anger
I ask God: *Are you there?* And He says, "Be Patient."

So I sulk, I withdraw, I get angry with God
"What kind of patience are you talking about? I could be patient and die of it." I whined
Finally with one desperate cry of surrender. I said to God: "I will be patient. Just speak to me."

Then God spoke to me: "When I say you should be patient, It's not because I hate you. It's not because I am indifferent to your pains.
But while you wait on me I put many things in place
I consolidate your answered prayer
I go ahead and deal with obstacles you'll face after you've had your desire granted.
I do not go to sleep, I am right beside you. I make all things beautiful in my time
I am never late, So don't be scared
You won't die before your answer comes
I give life and take it. So fear not!
You may not understand all of what I'm saying now
But with time, I know you will. It is always for your own good
That I say: Be Patient."

A Stitch in Time

A stitch in time saves nine
And make hay during the sunshine
Mama always made sure to say this
But I always waved it off with a hiss

One day my shirt had a pin-hole tear
And my shorts, a little eye at the rear
"Take thread, take needle" mama said
"And stitch them before you go to bed."
But omniscient, I thought I was
For I said to mama: "Why the fuss?"
"I'll manage it, I said to her
But I promise to stitch it later.

One thing here and another there
Events overtook my promise, oh dear
I still wore my shirt and short
But hoped mama wouldn't have me caught
I really thought I was smart
But I was as dumb as a doormat
Words of elders are words of wisdom
And heeding wise counsel brings us freedom

My shirt initially had a pin-hole tear
Which later took the size of a pear
My shorts had a little eye
Which ended up a small window. Oh why!
All these could have been avoided
If I'd listened to wise mama, the anointed
A stitch in time really saves nine
So please make hay during the sunshine

Chasing Shadows

Some things aren't real
They don't have a lasting value
They are like a mirage
Appearing inviting from afar
But on close observation
Is just an optical illusion.

But it's such things we choose to run after.
Wealth, fame, pleasure, selfish ambition
All offer some form of temporary comfort
But dependence on them
Is purely classical delusion.

Those things that last
Are things we do for others
Acts of love demonstrated to mankind
And efforts put into the service of God
Such, I say, will prove your total devotion.

On Your Way Up

I was well equipped on my way up
The hill was steep but I had the strength
I had a lot of food and drink
Which I shared with those I met.
"Thank you sir." They said to me
"we'll surely be of help sometime"
I smiled to myself as I heard those words
"That wouldn't be," I mumbled low

Soon my great strength began to fail
I who was strong now became weak
I couldn't go on, I began to slip
And worst of all my supplies were failing
Then some amazing things happened
That man I had earlier encouraged gave me some food
The woman I'd given some food to gave me water
Two children I had counseled showed me an easy path
One good turn surely deserves another

Nobody is useless
No one is insignificant
The person you despise today
May become great tomorrow
That little help you render today
Could very well speak for you someday
This is my advice, this is my counsel:
Do all you can for people on your way up
So that you may get help when your strength fails.

Stingy Sam

Stingy Sam. That was his name
So rich yet so tight-fisted and mean
He drove the kids away from his orchard
He yelled at the beggars by his gate
Such that they were too scared to return
He gave donations grudgingly and reluctantly
"They all want my money," He'd say to himself
As a result, people avoided him.

One day, however, he fell down the stairs
He was so stingy, he had no servant, no wife and no children
Stingy Sam didn't want to share his wealth
So he lay down there with no one to help
He was in pain, he needed friends
But they had chosen to stay away
He looked up to heaven and prayed to God:
"Lord Please help me and I'll change today"
God heard his cry and he rose a brand new man

I passed by his house the other day
There were kids on the fruit trees and beggars with lots of gifts
His friends are mainly needy people whom he helps
And they are always welcome in his home
He is married now with four children
We no longer call him Stingy Sam
He's now been christened Renewed Richie.

Are you one who enjoys wealth alone
Such that you're insensitive to others' needs?
Then let this story teach you before the hard lessons reach you
Wealth and fame are so easy to lose
Yet true friends are so hard to find
Don't be stingy, don't be mean
Learn to share and you won't regret.

They Celebrate His Death

There is a big celebration today
Someone has died, and they celebrate his death
In their part of the world
It is expensive for the relatives of the deceased
As they have to feed so many hungry mouths
They all came for the burial
At least, so it seems
But with the way they scramble for food and drink,
One wonders whether they came to pay the dead their last respect
Or just to eat and drink their last respect

As I stand appalled at what I see
As I see a reflection of their hearts through their actions
I conclude these people are only out to satisfy themselves....
To appease their gorge-like, insatiable appetite
Nobody is bothered about the dead anymore
Instead they want a goat, some more wine, more food
And they insist on camping in our family home
For three days, celebrating my father's death.

In this part of the world
It is expensive to live and more expensive to die
At the end of the burial I'm thoroughly exhausted,
My purse grown lean
Thankfully, my father won't die again

There is a big celebration today
My father has died,
And they celebrate his death.

Nobody Knows Me

Nobody knows me
disregarded, unknown, uncelebrated, despised
No one knows me
dejected, rejected, ostracized, humiliated
I wish they knew me
Castigated, slandered, intimidated, disdained
They still don't know me
Scorned, mocked at, oppressed, limited

So I worked on myself, painfully but gainfully
Until I attained a state of self discovery.
Now it doesn't matter anymore what anyone thinks
They may not know me
Belittled, maligned, back-stabbed and overlooked
But it's a non issue
Because now I know me.

Drug Abuse

She took a drag
The world suddenly went still
Then men became trees
She began to hear colors speaking
They spoke such beautiful words
Then as if that wasn't enough
She saw sounds chasing her.
The sound of a dog barking
seemed to wear a hat
And the sound of a baby crying
Seemed to wear a grim expression on its face.
This was becoming strange
She didn't understand.
She seemed to be in a different world
All the people there walked on their heads
The world was swirling.

Suddenly there was an earthquake
The world shook and flung people in different directions.
From left to right and from right to left.
The people seemed to be laughing
They seemed to be enjoying the joke

"The Joke?" She screamed.
"They're going nuts, they're going bunkers, they're going loco, they're going bananas. And oranges!"
Just then, she opened her eyes
And found herself in a gutter.
Little children were throwing stones at her.

"Oh! What a life," she soliloquized
She was a victim of drug abuse
And she couldn't help herself.
She needed counseling, she needed help.
She needed love and understanding.
But who was she to turn to?
Please could you help her?
And not just her, but all those drug addicts out there.
Would you please help?

The Beggar

There she sat....
Arms outstretched
Pleading for mercy
Begging for money
She sat on the floor
With a tree for backrest
The leaves above just managed
To shield her from the hostile sun

There she sat
Unspeaking, unseeing, unhearing, unwalking
Her heels designed with cracks
Plagued with wounds of no attention
From her body oozed a repulsive odor
An odor so strong that even flies avoided her
Her color darkened with dirt of neglect.

Still she sat
Motionless, arms outstretched
She was sleeping But her arms were trained.
Arms outstretched,
Rusty bowl by her left side
Into which landed those miserable coins, those pathetic looking notes.

Oh, poor beggar! Alone, blind, deaf, dumb, crippled
Only God is your comfort.
For no human being understands your pain,
your helplessness, your heart cry

There she sat
Day after day
Night after night
In the sun, in the rain
Days grew into weeks
Weeks matured into months
And months metamorphosed into years
There she sat
Year after year
Until the day she died

Back to Back

Back to back
We'll stand and fight
Greats warriors we
Cowards never be
Facing the enemy on both sides
We've got each other's back, low or high
None strikes your back
'Cos I'm there to hack
My back is safe
'Cos you're there to erase
We fight, disarm, put foe to flight
They try so hard till they lose their might

If you'd stood alone, you'd be dust by now
If I'd gone solo, I'd be down in an hour
But back to back
We kept our track
Defeated our fears
All through the years

Back to back we'll stand and fight
United we fly
Divided we die.

I Never Did It

I didn't know I had that much at my disposal
So I was careless
I Had a book that contained the information I needed
For my breakthrough
But it did not benefit me
Cos I never read it
It was just another addition
To my over-flowing-with-books library

I knew a man who could help me
But after sizing him up
I didn't even bother to tell him my problem
We met from day to day
But I just kept my worries to myself
I concluded that since he couldn't help himself
Then he couldn't help me
What I didn't know was that even though he couldn't help me
He knew someone who could
I was just a phone call away from transformation
But I blew it because I belittled my God-ordained helper.

I had so much knowledge in my head
But I felt it'd be of no use to anyone
I knew a lot, but I was ignorant of the fact that
What I knew could redeem someone else from ignorance
Does that sound complex?
Bottom line is this: appreciate whatever you have-
Friends, skill, knowledge, books, family etc
You may not know how valuable they are
Until despising them leads you to loss
Hope it doesn't get to that.

Too Busy to Love Her

I was too busy to love her
Even though I wanted to
My heart beats were punctuated
With loving thoughts I had of her
She never knew anyway
Because I was too busy to tell her
I was too busy to show her
I was too busy to smile at her
I was too busy to talk with her
Now I wonder who was more busy,
The busy bee or I?

I was too busy to love her
Even though the path for me was clear
I thought there'd always be time
To let her know of the love for her
That resonated within my stomach walls;
And ricocheted across my heart valve
So I kept on with my business
For I was too busy to love her
Now I wonder who was more busy
The busy bee or I?

I was too busy to love her
Even though I saw it in her eyes that she loved me
Even though I was confident she cared
I was careless, unappreciative of another's love
And I was taking her love for granted
I don't quite blame her for what happened afterwards
For while I was too busy to love her
Someone else wasn't
So I lost the love of my life to another
To a man who knew his priorities
Who was not too busy to love
Of course, she responded to his love
For we all want to be loved
Now all those things I was busy doing
Don't seem so important anymore
She deserved my love
But I didn't give it to her
Now I hear they are getting married
While I'm still here, appearing to be busy
Now I sit back and ask: who was more dumb
The Assyrian ass or I?

And So We Pray

I watched the politician. sly politician
He spoke so fluently, effortlessly, breathlessly
I've never heard a speech
So richly rhetoric
Full of allusions, insinuations, inflexions
Never beheld a delivery
So rich in theatrics, imagery and melodrama.
He spoke so beautifully
Bombastic, grandiloquent, pleonastic
And verbose he was.

Like a weaver bird,
He wove one tale into another
And as if the tales had life of their own,
Each tale dove-tailed into a philosophical saying
With rapt attention I followed
As he got himself entwined
In a labyrinth of his own lies and fables
Then with the Art of an escapologist
He meandered his way out of the oratorical mess
He'd got himself into

They hailed him.
"He is our man" they shouted
I stood there feeling sorry for the masses
Angry with the people who had brainwashed them
It's a pity that liars have become our role models,
Our representatives, our spokespersons
They apparently loved him. Or loved his money
So long as it was thrown around
I wasn't impressed, anyway
As sweet sounding as his words were
As appealing and soothing as they seemed
To the itchy ears that begged to hear them
The words were cacophonous to me
And I had drawn my conclusion:
He was just playing with words
And toying with the people's minds

And so we pray oh Lord
For men who will speak the truth
Without any cloud of deceit
Who will say what they mean
And mean what they say.

Leaders who will take us by the hand
And lead us to the land our fathers fought and died for
Who will lay down their lives, if need be
To protect their followers.
Lord we need real leaders
Not just professional orators.

I Can't Do It

I can't do it, I can't do it
That has been my creed in years gone by
Each time I was on the verge of defeat
I always backed out without a try

But my friend, I later learnt
That I could do anything no matter how great
Provided on doing it, I was bent
For life, dear one, is not hinged on fate

I'll let you in on something, if you please
It'll help you if you practice it
Never ever say: I can't
Cos you'll never get what you want

I can't means I admit defeat
Though the race is yet to begin
But you could have achieved the feat
If you had purposed in your heart, to win

Dare to explore your abilities
You'll be amazed at what's within you
For your challenges are like keys
That open doors of promotion for you.

Love Alive

Love is beyond words
It is almost indescribable
Love is the totality of God's nature
Love will do everything to uphold someone else
Love will do anything to make another
Better and greater
Love will say 'NO' uncompromisingly
If occasion demands
Love will not hesitate to be harsh or stern if need be
For it is not love to let your beloved go out of control
It is not love to let her go her own way and be destroyed

Love will jump at the opportunity
To discipline and chastise
If it can but save the life of the loved
Love does not hate the sinner
Rather it is the sin He hates
Love is not out to gain
Love is out to give
Love is not just romantic and sensual
Love is brotherly and inspirational
Love is not all words and no action

So put your love where your mouth is
Love will care for the sick and condole the bereaved
Love is so spiritual that it cannot neglect the physical
Love is not blind; love is kind
It's just that love chooses to overlook faults
Too bad we often mistake kindness for blindness,
Humility for stupidity; and calmness for madness
But true love is really hard to understand
Love is simply the greatest.

If you were given the privilege to choose
Between love and anything else
Choose love!
Love will make you free, but hatred will cage you
Love will lift your spirit but lust will leave you empty and hurt
Love will cast out fear but fear will becloud your love
Love without restriction
For you were made to love
Faith looks up to God, Hope looks ahead to God
But love takes you to God
For God is love.

Gone With the Wind

I had so many ideas
It was like a deluge
Like mighty waters breaking forth into the desert
I was fascinated with the feeling
Little insignificant me
Saturated with great goals, dreams and plans
They just kept coming.
And oh! How I loved the feeling
But I forgot one thing
Or perhaps, I didn't know how to do it
I didn't write down the ideas
And now? They're all gone
Gone with the wind.

I thought those ideas were exclusively mine
I expected them to know me, recognize me.
Their abode, their habitation
I thought they'd find their way back to me.
I thought I could recall them with a snap of my fingers
But I can't remember a tittle of them

Like an extinct sea creature
Those ideas have been washed away into oblivion
Save for the relics- the regret of not having
Written them down.

Justice

I believe in Justice
I loathe injustice
I will do anything to enforce justice-
Even go to war, if need be
I can't stand to see people deprived of it
That's why I joined the Justice Fraternity

Some multinational oil firms came to explore oil
And exploit my village
I was furious, so I got the brotherhood together
Me and my crew-The Justice Fraternity
I raised an army of fighters
Men who were as mad as myself…even madder
Mad at injustice and its practitioners
So we fought and maimed, wounded and killed
Destroyed and vandalized
All in a bid to exterminate injustice and enforce justice.

But as I take a look around my once peaceful village
Now war-torn and an ugly sight to behold
As I see the maimed, the bereaved and the dead
I wonder what the result of my war was.

True, I have enforced Justice
But will the maimed, bereaved and dead appreciate it?
Will justice bring back the dead or restore their mutilated bodies?
Will it restore my once serene village to its former state? NO!

There is a better way
Violence doesn't bring about justice
It brings pain, regret, retrogression and death
If we all learn to love
Be unselfish and considerate of our neighbors
If we live sacrificially
Then there'd be neither oppressor nor oppressed
Then and only then will Justice, equity and fairness prevail.

A Million Dollars

If I had a million dollars
I'll help everyone in need
I'll feed all the hungry people
I'll clothe all the naked
If only I had a million dollars….

If I had a million dollars
I'll become very generous and kind
I'll stop being tight-fisted as I am now
I'll support all those orphans and refugees
I've been hearing about for so long
Then I'll support the less privileged in their education
The world would really feel my impact
All I need is a million dollars….

This problem of poverty will be totally eradicated
I'll help all the poor people I meet
I'll pay the medical bills of the poor
I'll provide free drugs for them too
Dear God, only give me a million dollars….

Then God Spoke:

Last year I gave you a hundred dollars
You did nothing with it but buy yourself some clothes
Last month, I made someone give you a thousand dollars
You ended up buying a third car and marrying a fourth wife
Your late uncle left you five thousand dollars in his will
You did nothing with it but invite your friends for a party
Which cost a thousand dollars to organize
Then you took pleasure trips
around the world (even when people had needs around you)
You thought nothing about the orphanage two blocks away
You didn't think of your neighbor who has no job
Instead you spent your money recklessly
Until it was all gone

I would only give a million dollars to that man
Who has used his ten dollars wisely
He that is faithful in little
Is faithful also in much
If you touched no life with your ten, hundred or thousand dollars
Surely the same thing will happen if I gave you a million.

I'm Coming to the Top

I know you think I'm crazy
Or that I'm just dreaming.
But I mean every word of this—
'I'm coming to the top!'

I may not have much money now
Never mind my two shirts and one trouser
I know I'm still squatting with a friend
Somewhere in the ghetto
Okay, so what! Everybody knows I can't
Afford to eat well
It's very obvious from my pale face
And rather elongated neck.
But I dare say this today—
'I'm coming to the top!'

My dreams are bigger than me
And my vision, my pocket can't contain
But that's the way it should be
Else, we'd all die of stagnation.
Going by what I see now
It will be easier for an elephant

To pass through the eye of a needle,
Than for my dreams to come true.
But going by what I don't see
Going by God's promise,
I know my desires will come to pass.
My beginning is truly humble
I don't think any situation could be humbler
than mine right now
But I tell you what—
'I'm coming to the top!'

To the left and to the right,
Above, beneath and around
I sense this darkness…
Darkness of limitations, past failures,
Fear and doubt.
The darkness is so thick, I can almost
Touch it.
But I see through the darkness.
I see light, the light of God's word.
His word is a lamp, and His promise
Is a light.

Now I see!
I look beyond my present state
To what God says I will be.
My dreams and desires will be fulfilled,
The helplessness and hopelessness of
My present state, notwithstanding.
So with joy in my heart and full
Assurance of victory,
I yell—
'I'm coming to the top!'

The Invisible Limit

I can't really explain this
But let's hope my attempt to do so is successful.
There seems to be this force barring me from going astray…
Hindering me when I try to cross
The boundary, the dividing line…
It is an invisible limit.
I'm so blessed to be thus watched over.
For I do not stand by my might

When I attempt to do something wrong, for instance
I feel this check in my spirit is preventing me
Sometimes I'm about to say a filthy word,
Or pour out venomous words to hurt my fellow man
Or let out a stream of invectives,
But something stops me. I just do not find
The courage to speak on anymore.
At other times, I try to go some place
That will put a question tag on my faith.
But then, I feel that force again, preventing me.

People say I'm a saint, but I'm not.
I'm only preserved by the righteousness of another.
I'm standing because of he who keeps me from falling.
I am the righteousness of God through Christ.
So he keeps me in check by that invisible limit.
I must tell you, though that sometimes
I stubbornly and impetuously cross the limit.
I take advantage of liberty
I listen to my flesh and not HIS SPIRIT.
But then, over and over again,
His blood avails for me.
I plead for mercy.
I find my way back to my rightful place.
And I watch out, all the more carefully
So I do not cross again the boundary,
The invisible limit.

The Blunt Axe

My axe was blunt
My strength was gone
So I went to hunt
For a sharpening stone
I got some wood
It was cheap. What luck!
But it did no good
For my axe. Bad luck!

So I got a stone
A great big one
But my axe, dear one
Cut through the stone
I wanted to sharpen it-
My old blunt axe
Didn't want to test-run it
Or I'd be a dumb ass

But then it suddenly struck me
Iron, it is, that sharpens iron
Wood doesn't and stone, not really
So I got me a metal, a great big iron
To sharpen my axe, my old blunt axe
One, two, three, I counted. What a sight!
I quite agree I'd been a dumb ass
For my once blunt axe was as sharp as light

My message is this to you
As iron sharpens iron
So a man influences what his friends do
And as wood bows before iron
So bad friends should learn from the good.

What Your Hand Finds to Do

What your hand finds to do
Do with all your might
Do what you can while you can
For a day comes when you can't
I had many wonderful plans
But I always put them off for a better time
My wife was such a beauty within and without
She brought me joy and encouraged me in the service of God
I wanted to let her know how much I loved her,
Appreciated her help, cherished her company, her smile
But you see…I was waiting for the right time

My kids, three of them
Were gems of creation
They made a lot of noise, but I loved it
Their noise was like the sound of a tribe of red-Indians
Marking a special celebration
I loved each of them and wanted them to know it
I knew I needed to spend more time with them
But I was waiting for my magic moment

There were several books I could have written
Many people I could have helped
Several services I could have rendered
But I needed enough time, enough money, enough everything!
I kept postponing all those good things
Until the day I died.

Now my wife doesn't know how much I loved her
And my kids never got to know daddy more
The world has been robbed of hundreds of books
The poor have been deprived of a helper. What a loss!
Please make the best use of every opportunity
You might not have another

Santa Claus

Good old Santa
So kind and magnanimous
He is said to always carry a bag of presents
Which he distributes to people
Good old Santa, epitome of generosity

But must one wait until Christmas
To benefit from Santa? (For he only comes at Christmas)
Does that mean people will get no gifts
Until Christmas time?
I'll tell you what!
You can be Santa Claus to someone
You can share something with someone out there
You don't have to wait to receive from Santa
You can be the Santa someone is looking for

Give a gift, no matter how small
To any person, no matter how ordinary
With all your heart, no matter the day
Don't wait for Christmas to do good
So that someone can say:

"It isn't Christmas yet but I met Santa today
He gave me a gift, even though this is May
He gave me a place to stay
And I didn't have to pay
He saw me going astray
And he helped me find my way."

Money for Wedding

Peter used to think that finding a wife was a good thing
He felt that the wedding ceremony
Was the most desired experience in the world
But now he's beginning to have reservations.
Her father wants a motor-cycle
And the community wants four cows
The men are asking for ten kegs of palm wine,
Six cartons of beer, a ram and a bottle of foreign wine

The women are asking for two gallons of kerosene
And three bags of rice, supported with twelve tubers of yam
They say the bride's age mates want five rolls
Of an expensive cloth, and four crates of soft drinks
Her mother wants six yards of the latest fabric,
A pair of shoes, a bag to match, an umbrella and a grinder.

And for the wife to be?
Well, before the wedding, he needs to buy her a box of under wear,
Two leather boxes filled with clothes of all shades
The he must buy gold earrings and necklace
Finally, he needs to buy four pairs of shoes
And four handbags to match
All these fizzle into insignificance when

He thinks of the responsibilities that stare him in the face after marriage.
He'll need to take care of her sick father
He'll train her four brothers and three sisters
With her two cousins that her parents inherited
Then, he'll need to cope with the deluge
Of relatives who'd impetuously come
To take refuge in their home every month end
Waiting, like devourers, to consume
Whatever they can of his meager monthly stipend

Poor peter! Marriage is beginning to scare him
Starting to look like a yoke
Especially when he considers the attendant responsibilities
In any case, he doesn't have enough money yet.
He has not even drawn up a list of things he'll need
For the Church wedding
Each time he thinks of marrying this girl
His heart sinks to the pit of his stomach
Yet God's original plan is that anyone that finds a wife
Finds a good thing
I lend my voice to that of Peter
I present a plea to his in-laws to be
Could you please be less cruel?

I Want to Serve You

I left home that morning, a quarter to eight
"Church starts by eight," I thought, "and look, I'll be late."
"I want to serve you Lord, today." I prayed
As I walked hurriedly along the way.
On my way, I saw this man
Quite untidy with unkempt hair
"Please sir, I need your help. Help me sir, I need your help."

"Alas, poor man" I said to him
I haven't a minute and I'm very late
"May God take control," I hurriedly said
While I walked off with no backward glance
After service (of course I was late),
I decided to pass by the way I came
And there I saw that poor old man
All beaten up and left to die.

I later found he needed food
Which none was willing to give to him
Even I who claimed to love God
Didn't as much as ask his need
I rushed to his side, he smiled at me

"No one would help so I had to steal
You wanted to serve a great, big, God
But wouldn't help a poor needy man
How could you serve God, yet ignore me?"
He prayed-"oh Lord, forgive my sins"
And with a smile he lay back dead.

I felt so sad, I felt so bad
How would you feel if you were me
If you want to serve God indeed
Start with that fellow who needs your help
And someday God will say to you,
"When you served your fellow man, you truly served me."

My Five Stones

He had never lost a battle
He was terror to his foes
His name sent shivers through the anatomy of his enemies
The thought of him alone had them transfixed like monoliths
His name was Goliath of Gath.

I too had never lost a battle
I was a terror to my foes
My presence sent shivers through the system
Of lions and bears
But brought a sense of security to my sheep
I had killed a Lion and bear, though never a man.
Yet the courage, resilience and sense of responsibility
My shepherd boy job gave me
Would see me through greater challenges
My name is David, Son of Jesse.

He looked down at me, debasingly, disdainfully, derogatorily
I looked up at him with Faith in my God,
Fire in my soul and fear thrown away
Then I reached into my bag and drew out
One of the five smooth stones in there

My five stones stood for F-A-I-T-H
They stood for D-A-V-I-D
And they stood for J-E-S-U-S
I, David, needed Faith in Jesus

He spoke arrogantly, debasing me in the process
But I knew even though he be mighty like a mountain
My God was mightier than the mountains.
So I spoke, debasingly, to him too
"I'll cut off your head and give to the birds." I said
Then I put the stone in the sling and let it go
There was silence…then pandemonium
As the philistines took to their heels
An unbelievable, unthinkable, unimaginable thing had happened
Goliath, the philistine was dead!
My stone got him in the forehead
And he fell down with a loud thud

I who was once unknown became a warrior
We become warriors when we face and overcome our challenges
You too are a potential warrior
But you can never fully become one

Until you confront those things you've been evading
Until you face squarely those issues
You've been running away from
Put that stone in the sling and let it go
If it's done with Faith in Jesus
Then watch out! For Goliath falls in a heap.

Evasive Emmy

He always sat on the fence
I can't remember ever seeing him
On either side of the fence
"it's safer for me," he'd usually say
"I can flee to any side in the event of danger."

But one day, the fence collapsed
And my friend, Emmy, was caught off guard
He went down with the fence and broke his back
He tried to avoid the fall, he really did
But you can't do that sitting on the fence

As long as you don't decide which side you're on
As often as you avoid taking a decisive stand
You remain stagnant and stuck
You stand the risk of falling with the fence
And breaking your back like Evasive Emmy
By the way, he still carries a scar on his back today
He's lucky he can walk again
But he has never sat on the fence after that great fall
He's always on one side or the other.

Be Nice to People

I met this fellow with worn out clothes
I didn't think he was worth a dime
I treated him as I did my goats
I didn't think he was worth my time

In place of a hot meal, I gave him a cold one
Food on the floor not on the table
Treated him like dirt and thought it was fun
But times and seasons are unpredictable

By that I mean a time will come
When the poor and lowly will become great
And men now with a pathetic form
Will someday walk with royal gait

Well that was years ago
But now, that fellow is very rich
To the wind has flown my ego
For he has prospered far beyond my reach

How I wish I could change the past
I wish I had treated him well then
For now the first has become last
And the last, respected among men.

Mr Overtaker

He was an over taker
He rode a bike, the over taker
He loved to overtake every time
And felt he'd get away with it anytime
He went past my car. Pathological over taker
But ahead was a trailer

Mr. over taker was doing well
Until we got to a sharp bend
That for him would have been the end
If not for the mud into which he fell
If you had hit the pavement, Mr. Over taker
We'd probably have had to call the undertaker

He didn't succeed in overtaking the trailer
And I went past the overtaken over taker
With my car which he felt was too slow
The trailer driver offered to give him a tow
Poor over taker! Impatient rushaholic
I'd rather you were a workaholic
Friend, hope you get the point I make
Learn to be patient so your bones don't break.

Divided We Fall

United we stand, divided we fall
If we don't work together
We'll soon come up against a brick wall
If you want to be a pacesetter
Then into the line of unity you must fall
For then only will you get better and better
And probably make it to Fame Hall.

United we win, divided we lose
If you insist on taking the glory alone
You'll be hanging other people with a noose
And you shouldn't think you'd be left alone
For every sponsor of division pays his dues
Pain and regret for the seed he has sown
Even if he decides to sleep on church pews

United we stand, divided we fall
The enemy knows and so he tries
To stop us from heeding this call-
The call to unity and fraternal ties
So now, in your court is the ball
Which do you choose, to be foolish or wise?
For united we stand, divided we fall.

Not Afraid to Die

I'm not afraid to die
Why should I be?
Jesus has died for me
So I'm delivered from the second death
I'm safe in God's arms
When He calls me, I'll go
I pray that by then
I'll have fulfilled His plans for my life
Completed the task He gave me
I pray that I'd have affected the lives
I was ordained to affect

I'm not afraid to die
I only pray that it won't be premature
For I worry about my pretty wife
And beloved children
I can't stand to think of the pain
They'll go through if I leave…..
Oh God! On that note, I think I'm a little afraid

But I'm not afraid to die
I really am not
If I happen to leave them
God will take care of them
He will be husband to my wife
And father to my children
He will raise people to continue the work
From where I stop
On that account, I'm not afraid to die!

Talk to Me

I wish I could read your mind
I really wish I could
Sometimes I think you're trying to say something
Or is it, trying not to say something?
I stare at your lips, they only tremble slightly
I look into your eyes and all I see is that cold, blank, expressionless gaze.
So I act based on what I see
I never knew you loved and cared about me
Because you never told me so
You think I should have known you loved me
But I think you should know I didn't know
If only you had told me
I'd have responded with love, not callous apathy.

I didn't understand your intentions
I had my preconceived ideas
I went in for the kill and mercilessly attacked you with accusations
But you were innocent
You did what you did in my own interest
But I felt you had something else on your mind
So I considered you selfish, inconsiderate and mean
Now I'm ashamed to admit I was the jerk

All I should have done was to ask you in polite terms
And we'd have avoided this trouble
All you should have done was to let me know
Why you acted the way you did
I couldn't read your mind

Please let me know what's on your mind and I'll do the same
That way we'd minimize the friction and misunderstanding
We'll understand, know and love each other more
"There's no art to tell the mind's construction on the face." Says the sage
So tell me what you think, how you feel
Even if it hurts or breaks my heart
I can bear it, I will bear it
Knowing what you think is certainly better
Than being kept in the dark
So let me into your mind
Please talk to me!

Colourful But Weak

I went out one day
To buy me some furniture
So I searched all day
For chairs, steady and sure

The first set I saw
Didn't look so colorful
The color didn't fit my floor
I needed something more wonderful

The second set I found
Was sound, strong and solid
But I wouldn't part with a pound
I wanted something more florid

At last I went for a set
All colorful but average in strength
I felt it was the best
So for it I happily went

Back home I came to discover
That my chairs were colorful but weak
Boy! I'm still trying to recover
From the greatest shock of the weak

For as I lowered myself
Into my colorful chair
Behold I found myself
Sprawled on the floor. Oh dear!

Never ever go for just color
At the expense of durability and quality
For some bad things are wrapped in color
Do not become a casualty

Now when I go to buy anything
I touch, I think, I ask, I test
All so I don't buy just anything
For it may turn out to be colorful dirt.

Just a Little More

Many years ago
I sat on an old wooden stool
It was the only piece of furniture
In my almost-bare room
Yet I treasured it like a woman would treasure
Her diamond ring
I was poor and miserable
So poor that even the poor called me poor
I was tagged 'king of paupers' in the ghetto where I lived

I didn't have a bicycle
So don't even think of a car
All I could boast of was my old, wooden stool
And even that was weak and worn with age
Having originated from my great grand father
I must confess though, that I had food to eat, few clothes to wear
Ad a roof over my head, even though it was rusty and leaking
Well, I said to God: "If only I had a little more, I'll be happy."
So I worked and worked
I toiled and moiled
I wanted to earn a little more. Just a little more
So I'd be happy and satisfied

Some years after that, I sat on some fairly comfortable seats
In my two-bedroom apartment
I had a motorcycle and a growing business
I wasn't married yet
But I must confess that I had enough food to eat
Several changes of clothes and a roof over my head
But I wasn't satisfied
So I whispered to God: "If only I had a little more, I'll be happy."
So I worked much harder
I labored, I slaved, I hustled and struggled
All in a bid to lay hold of happiness and satisfaction
But the closer I approached, the farther happiness seemed
To go away from me
I desperately wanted to have all I needed to make me comfortable,
Happy and satisfied
Such that I lost a lot of friends in the process- and my peace of mind too

Again some years later, I sat on a set of exquisite leather chairs
I had succeeded in building a mansion at a high-brow area of our town
Yes! I was part of the crème-de-la-crème. The town shakers!
I had a wife and four children who had the best of everything
And that is not an understatement!

I must tell you, though, that we had more than enough to eat,
Extra clothes, which we didn't get to wear in a long while
And a beautiful roof, with custom made ceiling
I know you think a man like that should be satisfied. But guess what?
That thing stirred up within me once more
And I found myself saying: "If only I had a little more, I'll be happy."

Many of you are just like me
Struggling to find happiness in the corridors of the great
I passed through those corridors once and quite a number of people
I met there were great but miserable
They were good looking and desirable from the outside
But were wretched, unfulfilled and empty on the inside
No amount of possessions or money
Will make you happy and fulfilled
There'll always be something within you
Crying for a little more and you could spend your whole life,
All your productive days, trying to get that 'little more.'

What I just told you happened years ago
But today I'm fulfilled, happy and satisfied
I didn't find peace in my possessions,
I found peace and joy in God
I've learnt to be grateful for the little I have and God has kept blessing me
More and more
It's worth knowing that I seek God first now and all those other things
I desire are added to me
Godliness with contentment, we are told, is great gain
I no longer say: "I wish I could have a little more."
Instead I ask God: "What do you want me to do with what you've given me?"
"Whose life can I possibly affect with what I have?"
Well even at that, I still have enough food to eat, clothes to wear,
And good shelter
I'm a changed man now and I hope you'll grow up too and stop saying,
Like I used to: "If only I had a little more, I'll be happy."

CPSIA information can be obtained
at www.ICGtesting.com
Printed in the USA
BVHW072106081019
560550BV00001B/18/P